A Mirror, a Carpet & a Lemon

Retold by Jenny Dooley

Primary Stage 3 Teacher's Edition

Express Publishing

Published by Express Publishing

Liberty House, New Greenham Park, Newbury,
Berkshire RG19 6HW
Tel.: (0044) 1635 817 363
Fax: (0044) 1635 817 463
e-mail: inquiries@expresspublishing.co.uk
http://www.expresspublishing.co.uk

Colour Illustrations: Terry Wilson

First published 2002

ISBN 1-84325-776-9

CONTENTS

Introduction

Storytime is a series of graded readers which is aimed at young learners between the ages of 6 and 10. The series helps students to develop their knowledge of the English language through enjoyable stories which have been carefully selected from all over the world. The series also provides further practice of the language presented in each story. Therefore, it is suitable for use as a supplement to most primary courses and in all teaching situations.

The books are especially designed to motivate young learners of English as a foreign language and encourage them to take an active interest in the language. Each story can easily be turned into a play for a class production. These plays offer parts to learners of different abilities and are therefore suitable for all primary classes.

The series has three key levels:

Primary Stage 1 ***Primary Stage 2*** ***Primary Stage 3***

The stories are written in rhyme for ***Primary Stages 1*** and ***2***, as learners aged 6 to 9 tend to find it much easier and more enjoyable to read and learn language in rhyme; ***Primary Stage 3*** has been written in prose, as learners at this stage should be exposed to everyday speech patterns. Each story is accompanied by a fully-dramatised recording, so that even learners who use the series outside the classroom can benefit from exposure to the correct pronunciation and intonation of the English language. In addition, they will gain a better understanding of the language in context.

Storytime Primary Stage 3 is the last stage of the series. It is designed for children between the ages of 9 and 10 who have completed between 150 and 180 hours of English language learning.

Components:

- Pupil's Book
- Teacher's Edition
- Audio CD / Cassette

The ***Pupil's Book*** is divided into five main sections:

- The story itself is presented in double-page spreads and is accompanied by a picture dictionary for each spread, which presents the core vocabulary used.
- Activities for further practice of the language learned throughout the story. These are clearly indicated in the main story through child-friendly signposting.
- Songs related to the main topic of each scene.
- A script and a list of props for the production of the story as a play. This will activate the students' passive language by encouraging its use in a real situation (the staging of the play). It will also help teachers by illustrating how the play can be staged simply and effectively.
- An alphabetical wordlist of all the vocabulary items presented in the picture dictionary throughout the story. This may easily be turned into a glossary if the students are encouraged to write their first language equivalent next to each item.

The ***Teacher's Edition*** includes all of the above, the only difference being that the answers in the *Activities* section are over-printed for easy reference. It also includes an additional section called *Suggestions for Staging* which offers stage directions, practical tips on costuming, floor plans, a list of props needed for each scene (as well as ideas on how to make them) and drama activities so that learners are prepared and motivated to take part in the production.

Suggested Lesson Plan

The story can be covered in five lessons. Each lesson has a corresponding set of tasks in the *Activities* section.

In the first lesson:
When first presenting the story, start by brainstorming ideas on the subject of the story by asking questions about the title and the cover of the book. If necessary, allow students to use their mother tongue to answer the questions.
e.g. *What is the title of this story?*
What can you see in this picture?
What are they doing?
What do you think this story is about? etc

In all lessons:

1. As an introduction to the lesson, pre-teach the core vocabulary. Then focus on the main scenes in each spread and ask questions to help students describe the action in the pictures.
   e.g. *Who is this?* (point to each character in turn)
   What is he/she doing?
   What do you think is happening here?
2. Play the recording for the whole lesson. Students follow in their books.
3. Ask students questions about the action in the story and whether it was as they expected.
4. Play the recording again, pausing at the end of each line to allow students to repeat. Repeat this step as many times as necessary. Instruct students to do the same at home with their own recording so as to improve their ability to read aloud as well as to practise their intonation and pronunciation.
5. Assign roles and ask students to read the story aloud in class. Repeat this step until every student has had an opportunity to read.
6. Revise the core vocabulary which was pre-taught in step 1.
7. Point to the signpost referring students to the *Activities* section for that lesson. Ask them to turn to these activities in the book. Go through the activities in class, without allowing students to write the answers. Assign them as written homework.
8. Play the song at the end scene and ask the class to practise singing it along with the CD/cassette.

In the next lesson:

1. Start by asking questions to revise the story so far. These can be answered in the students' mother tongue.
2. Assign students a role in the story and ask everybody to read the story aloud. Demonstrating what students have learnt at home will enhance their confidence and motivate them to continue with their learning. Make sure you always give them some positive feedback on their performance whether it is on their pronunciation or acting.
3. Proceed to the next lesson in the story.

Song

A Faraway Land!

Our story starts in a palace with towers,
with beautiful gardens full of birds and flowers.
Princess Perihan lives in this land,
and everyone wants to win her hand.

Princes bring gifts from everywhere,
to show her dad how much they care.
But in this story you will see
what the greatest gift can be!

Sultan

daughter

marry

competition

Once upon a time there was a Sultan
who had a beautiful daughter.
Her name was Perihan and she was so beautiful
that birds would start singing
when she walked through the gardens.
Princes everywhere wanted to marry her.
But the Sultan loved his Perihan very much
and he could not choose between the princes.
So one day, he thought of a competition.

a gift

the world

golden feathers

a palace

carry

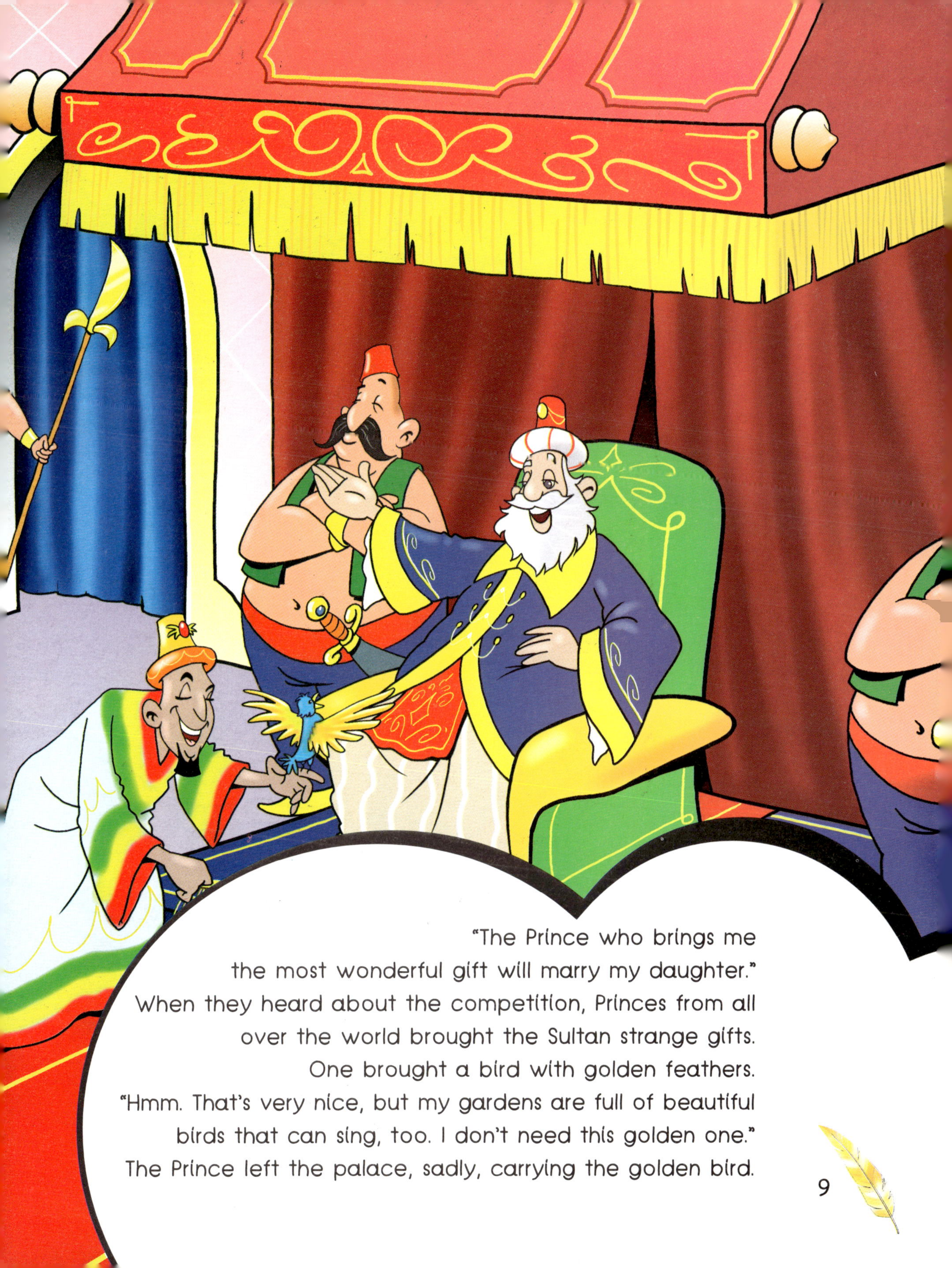

"The Prince who brings me
the most wonderful gift will marry my daughter."
When they heard about the competition, Princes from all
over the world brought the Sultan strange gifts.
One brought a bird with golden feathers.
"Hmm. That's very nice, but my gardens are full of beautiful
birds that can sing, too. I don't need this golden one."
The Prince left the palace, sadly, carrying the golden bird.

a hen

colourful eggs

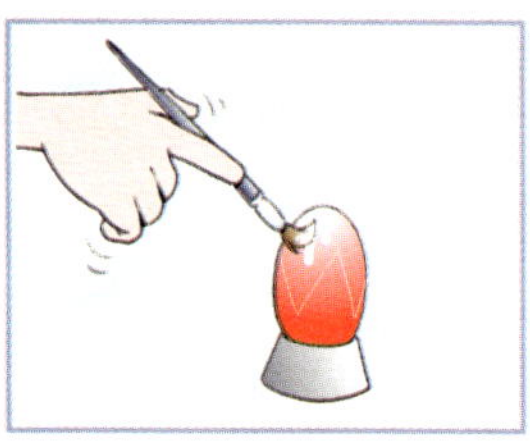

paint

Another brought a hen that could lay colourful eggs.
"What use do I have for colourful eggs?
If I want blue eggs or red eggs, I can just paint them!"
said the Sultan.

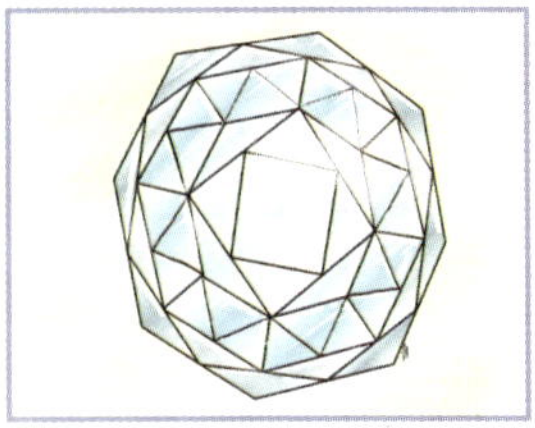

a diamond

the shape of a star

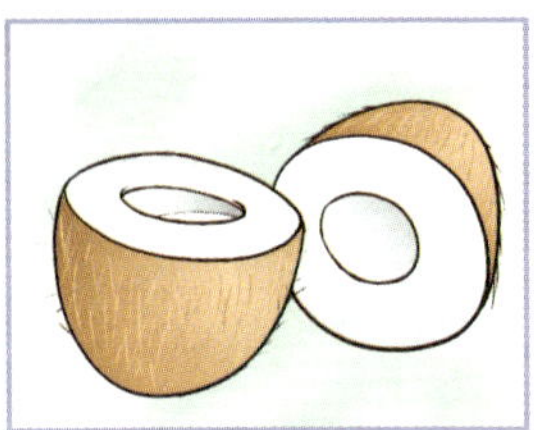

coconut

sparkling

precious jewels

Another brought a diamond in the shape of a star and as big as a coconut. The Sultan took the Prince to a big room, opened the door, and the Prince saw sparkling diamonds everywhere.

"As you can see, I have more diamonds and precious jewels than I need."

Activities A-C

"They are all wonderful gifts.
But none of them are special enough
to let you marry my daughter."
And all the Princes left, sadly.

Song

What Can We Offer the Sultan?

What can we offer the Sultan?
We brought him the best we can find!
But nothing is better than what he has got.
We think he is very unkind!

What can we offer the Sultan?
I can't believe what I heard!
He's not impressed with the golden feathers
of my beautiful golden bird!

What can we offer the Sultan?
A magical hen is just great!
If you want red, green or blue eggs,
you've got them right there on your plate!

What can we offer the Sultan,
when diamonds are not good enough?
He's got more than a jewellery shop
and lots of other stuff!

a land

hear

gold

a market

strange things

In another faraway land, there lived three brothers, who were Princes.
They, too, heard of Princess Perihan's beauty and they all wanted to marry her. Each of them had five thousand pieces of gold to buy a gift for the Sultan. So they went to a market full of strange things to find gifts.

magic

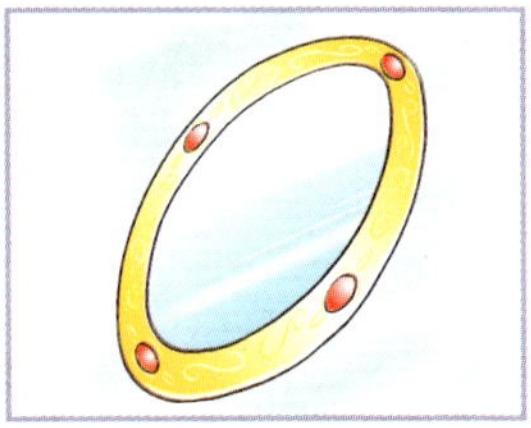

a mirror

see

The first Prince bought a magic mirror. In it you could see what was happening anywhere in the world! "This is the most wonderful gift of all! Surely the Sultan will let **me** marry his daughter!"

a carpet

sit

fly

The second Prince bought a magic carpet.
When you sat on it,
you could fly anywhere in the world!
"This is a fantastic gift!
I will be the one to marry the Princess!"

Activities D-E

a merchant

a lemon

juice

In the market, the third Prince, the youngest of all, saw a merchant whom he had never seen before. "Lemons! Lemons!" the merchant called. The Prince was interested and asked the merchant what was special about his lemons. "These are **magic** lemons! The juice from them will cure any illness!"

think

The merchant told the Prince
each lemon cost five thousand pieces of gold.
The Prince thought for a long time.
"Maybe this gift will be the one the Sultan likes."
And he paid five thousand pieces of gold
for one small lemon!

Song

The Best Gift For Love!

With a magic mirror,
you can see your true love's face,
even if they're far away
in another place.

The magic carpet
takes you to your true love's heart -
in just a minute you are there,
no matter how far apart.

A magic lemon
cures you and makes all sick things well.
Which of these gifts is the best,
I wonder? Can you tell?

a journey

good-better-best

1 = first
2 = second
3 = third

laugh

The next day, the three Princes began their journey to the Sultan's palace. They all talked about their gifts.

"Mine is the best gift! I will marry the Princess!"

"My magic carpet is better than your magic mirror! I will marry the Princess!"

"No, I will marry the Princess! I have a wonderful lemon!"

The first and second Princes laughed and laughed.

"He paid five thousand pieces of gold for one lemon!"

"And now **he** thinks he will marry the Princess!"

look into

cry

by her bedside

die

take

"What do you think the Princess looks like?"
"I know! I will look in my magic mirror!"
So the three Princes looked
into the magic mirror and what did they see?
The beautiful Princess was lying on her bed looking
very ill, and her father was crying by her bedside.
"Oh no! She's dying!"
"Quick, let's go!
My magic carpet can take us to the palace!"

Activities F-G

Song

Fly Us Away!

Oh magic carpet, fly us away!
We don't want to be late!
Please hurry, hurry, don't delay!
Take us to Perihan's gate!

Oh magic carpet, fly us away,
over deserts made of sand.
Please hurry, hurry, don't delay!
Fly us to Perihan's land!

jump onto

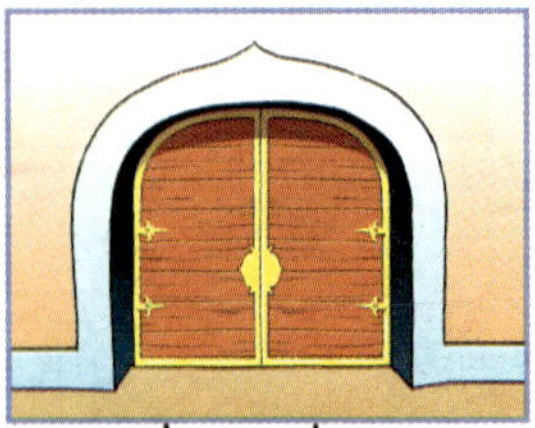

palace doors

a hall

step forward

help

a doctor

The three Princes jumped onto the magic carpet.
In one minute, they were at the Sultan's palace!
The three Princes walked through the big palace doors.
In the hall, they saw the Sultan sitting on a sofa, crying.
"My poor daughter! My beautiful Perihan!"
The third Prince stepped forward and said,
"Your Majesty, I can help your daughter."
"Our best doctors have tried to cure Princess Perihan and they failed! How can **you** save her?" said the royal doctor.
"Oh let him try! Anything for my beautiful Perihan!"

follow

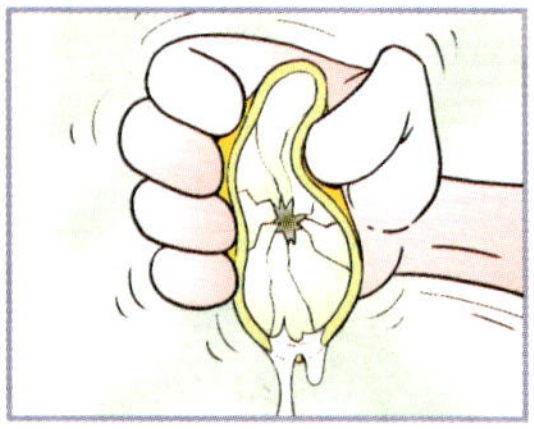

squeeze

pink cheeks

shout

hug

The three Princes followed the Sultan to a room where Perihan lay on her bed, looking very ill. The youngest Prince squeezed the lemon and gave a cup of the juice to the Princess. After a minute, her cheeks became pink again. She got up and ran into her father's arms. "Perihan, you are well again!" shouted the Sultan and hugged his daughter! He could not believe his eyes!

turn to

Then he turned to the Princes and asked
them why they had come to the palace.
"To marry the Princess!"
said all three Princes at the same time.
"I have a magic mirror! You can see anywhere
in the world in it. I looked into it and saw
Princess Perihan was ill. I should marry the Princess!"
"But, my flying carpet got us here in one minute!
It can take you anywhere you want to go,
so I think I should marry the Princess!"

Activities H-J

both

"They are both very special gifts, thank you,"
said the Sultan and turned to the third Prince.
"Now, what have **you** brought?"
"I brought this lemon," the third Prince said and gave
the Sultan the squeezed lemon.
His brothers laughed but Perihan did not.
She asked her father which was the best gift.
"Well ... the magic mirror and the flying carpet
are both very interesting ... "

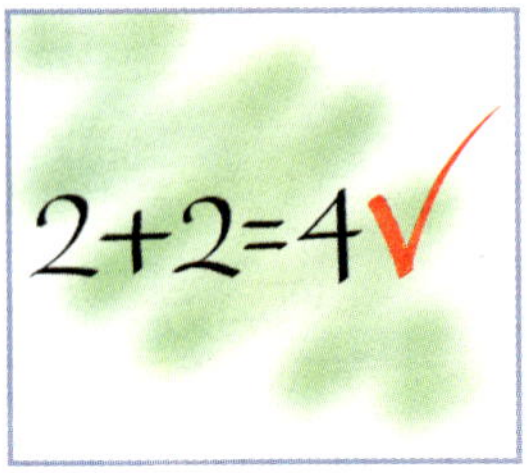

right

"Yes, Father. They **are** interesting gifts,
but the lemon is the best gift of all. It saved my life!"
"You're right, Perihan! Life is the most precious gift of all.
The youngest Prince **should** marry my daughter!"
And that is how a simple lemon won
the Sultan's daughter - beautiful Princess Perihan.
And they all lived happily ever after.

Activities K-M

Song

Life is the Best Gift of All!

We can give jewels and diamonds,
and other gifts to our friends.
But some things are more important
to us all in the end.

Chorus: What use are jewels and diamonds,
if you haven't got a wife?
What use is silver and gold?
The best gift of all is life!

There are some things we can't buy,
no matter how much we've got.
And life is the most precious gift
of all, no matter what!

Repeat chorus

ACTIVITIES

Activities for pages 6-13

A Look and write.

0 

S u l t a n

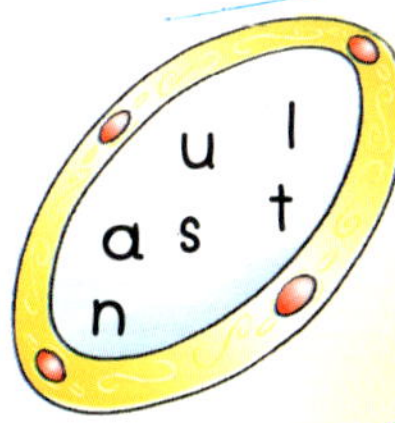

1 

f e a t h e r s

2 

d a u g h t e r

3 

d i a m o n d

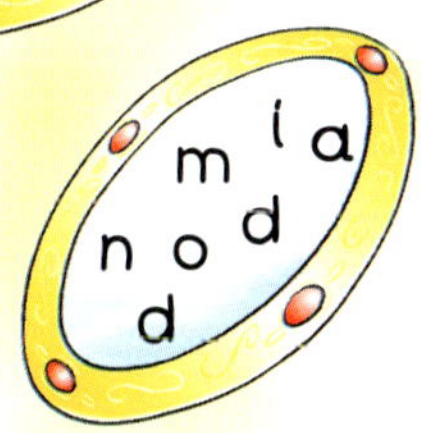

4 

c o c o n u t

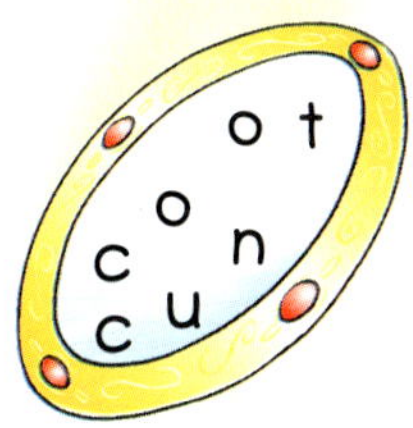

B Look and match.

0

1

2

3

4

5

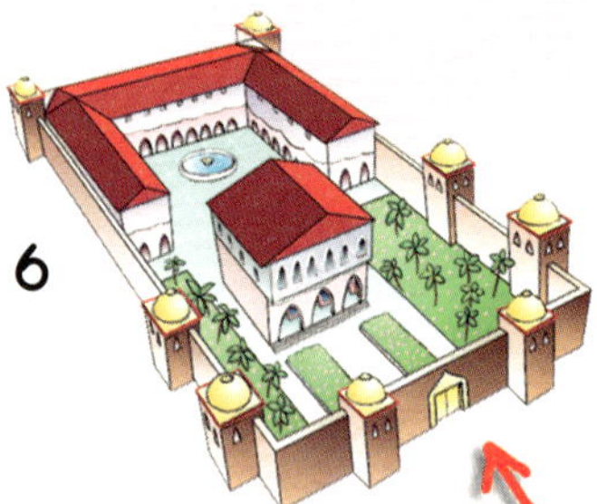

6

competition

gift

palace

jewels

star

prince

world

C Read and underline.

0 wonderful gifts / gold

1 precious jewels / coconut

2 colourful princes / eggs

3 golden feathers / Sultan

4 sparkling competition / diamonds

Activities for pages 14 - 23

D Look, read and circle.

0 

a world
b land

1 

a market
b palace

2 

a coconut
b carpet

3 

a star
b gold

4 

a mirror
b diamond

5 

a hen
b eggs

E Look, read and put a tick (✓) or a cross (✗).

0  It's a coconut. ✗

1  It's a competition. ✗

2 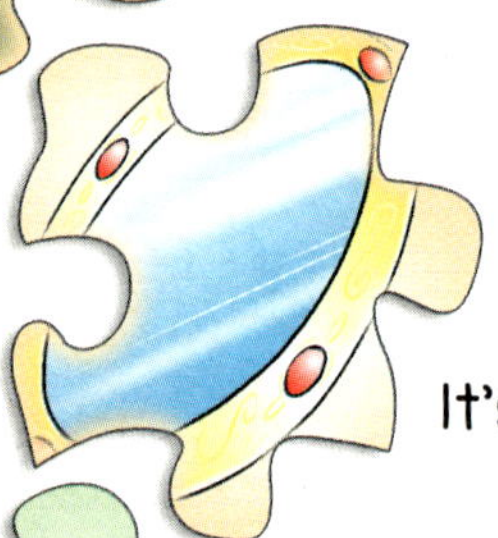 It's a mirror. ✓

3  It's a diamond. ✗

4  It's a feather. ✓

5  It's a market. ✗

Activities for pages 24 - 33

F Look, read and match.

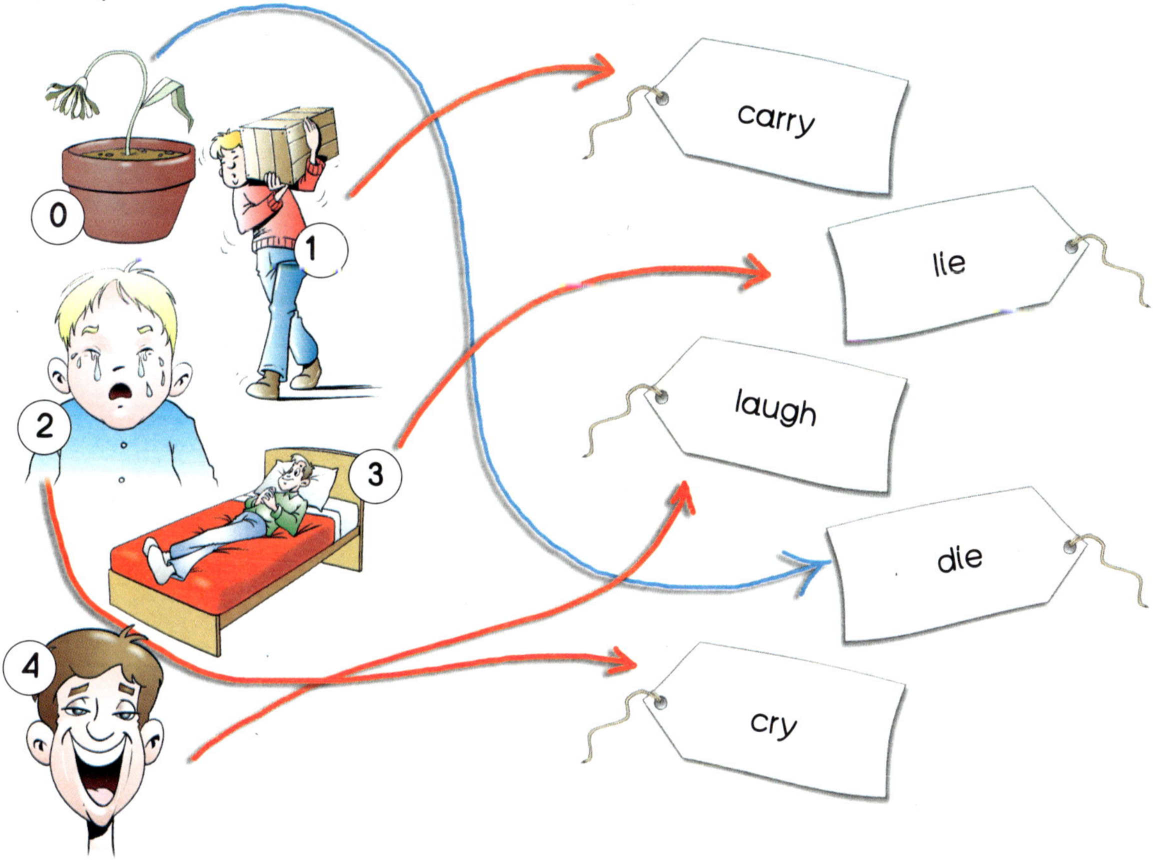

G Find the adjectives: colourful, good, better, best, first, second, third, ill, golden, sparkling, precious.

C	O	L	O	U	R	F	U	L	G
G	O	N	U	T	H	I	R	D	O
S	E	C	O	N	D	R	Z	I	O
T	W	N	Y	B	E	S	T	A	D
I	L	L	B	E	T	T	E	R	I
M	X	P	R	E	C	I	O	U	S
S	P	A	R	K	L	I	N	G	A
G	O	L	D	E	N	D	K	S	K

Activities for pages 36 - 41

H Look at the pictures and write the words.

0 juice

1 merchant

2 doctor

3 both

4 hall

5 palace doors

I Look and write: turn to, look into, jump onto, step forward.

0 turn to

1 jump onto

2 step forward

3 look into

J Look at the pictures and complete the sentences.

0 He is ......shouting...... .

1 It is ......flying...... .

2 She is ......thinking......

3 He is ...helping... the man.

4 He is ...taking... the boy to school.

5 It is ...following... the boy.

6 She is ...hugging... her teddy bear.

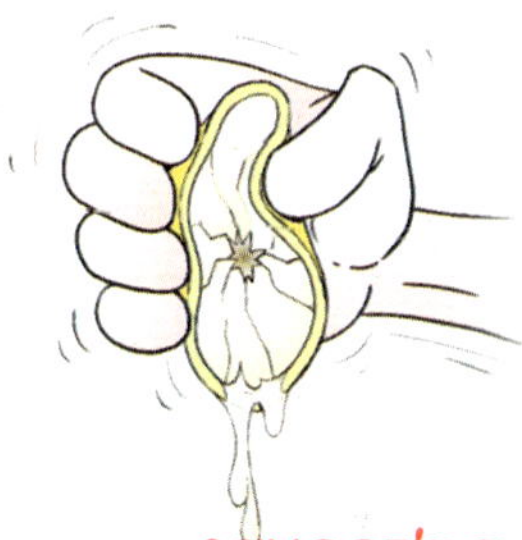

7 He is ...squeezing... a lemon.

8 He is ...sitting... on a carpet.

Activities for the whole story

K Who said it? Listen, read and match.

a "The Prince who brings me the most wonderful gift will marry my daughter."
b "As you can see, I have more diamonds and precious jewels than I need."
c "The juice from them will cure any illness!"
d "My magic carpet is better than your magic mirror."
e "Your Majesty, I can help your daughter."
f "Yes, Father. They are interesting gifts but the lemon is the best gift of all."

1 The Sultan ....a.... , ...b....
2 The merchant ....c....
3 Princess Perihan ....f....
4 The third Prince ....e....
5 The second Prince ....d....

L Fill in the crossword and find the secret sentence.

What's the secret sentence?

It saved my life!

M Read and colour the picture.

The three Princes are in Princess Perihan's bedroom. It's a pink bedroom with a large purple bed and a blue carpet next to it. The first Prince is carrying a red carpet and he is wearing yellow clothes. The Prince with the mirror is wearing green clothes and the third Prince is wearing orange clothes. They are all looking at Princess Perihan and the Sultan. The Sultan is wearing blue clothes and the Princess is wearing a pink dress.

Suggestions for Staging

How to stage the play

Each production of the "A Mirror, a Carpet and a Lemon" play can be adapted according to the space and facilities available for the performance. Below is a plan of the theatre used for the author's production.

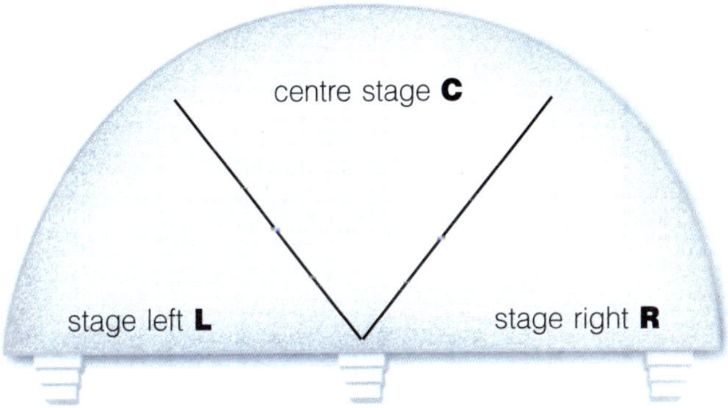

For the purposes of the play, the narration may be performed by the older students in the class. They can share the lines between them. It is suggested that they hold the entire script with their own lines highlighted. To add to the atmosphere, they can be dressed as genies but should always remain at the side of the stage, either on the left or on the right.

After completing all the lessons in "A Mirror, a Carpet and a Lemon", students should have a clear idea of the story and the accompanying action, but another reading of the script will help everyone visualise the play on stage. This reading will also provide a perfect opportunity for the teacher to explain the differences between a story and a play and to decide on the allocation of roles or any other changes that might be appropriate. If there are any shy students who are reluctant to act, they can still be involved in the production by collecting / making props, being prompters (for those who forget their lines), setting up the stage or playing the cassette / CD with the final song etc.

Once the roles are allocated and the students know which characters they are playing, they can use the recording to practise their lines and cues at home. In class, details such as the way actors move, speak, enter or exit etc, can be discussed at the beginning of each rehearsal. Then, the actors can rehearse and get feedback from the teacher on their performance. It is a good idea for the final song to be performed by a different group of students, singing along with the cassette / CD. This will boost their confidence and encourage them to perform in front of a live audience.

Before each rehearsal, it is advised that the students carry out one of the drama activities suggested in this book, which are designed to relax and motivate the students in preparation for the rehearsal ahead. The activities involve movement, mime, voice and expression, and are aimed at familiarising the students with the basics of drama.

Finally, before the performance, it is a good idea to have at least one dress rehearsal, in which the actors should be in costume and the remaining 'backstage crew', i.e. prompters, stage assistants, sound assistants etc, should be ready to await their cues.

Script and General Stage Directions

The number of roles in this play can easily be adapted to fit the number of students available or willing to take part. For example, all the narrator's parts can be performed by one student or they can be divided by the teacher into more parts if necessary. The narrator(s) should be dressed in a way suitable to the theme of the play. In this instance, they could be dressed as genies. Narrators should always stand on the left or the right of the stage in such a way that they do not interfere with the action or obstruct the view of the audience.

Actors: The Sultan
The Sultan's Guard
The Three Suitors
The Three Merchants
The Three Princes
The Royal Doctor
Princess Perihan

Narrators: 1 or as many Ss as necessary, dressed as genie(s).

> In the script there are a number of coloured, optional lines given to some roles which you can use if you want to give students more to do on stage. These lines sometimes repeat information already given by the Narrator. You may decide that you want to change some of the Narrator's lines to avoid this repetition.

***Song* - A Faraway Land!**

Our story starts in a palace with towers,
with beautiful gardens full of birds and flowers.
Princess Perihan lives in this land,
and everyone wants to win her hand.

Princes bring gifts from everywhere,
to show her dad how much they care.
But in this story you will see
what the greatest gift can be!

Scene 1

Curtains open. Stage lights on. The Sultan is sitting on his throne, centre stage, with his chin resting on his hand, deep in thought. There is a picture of Princess Perihan on the backdrop.

Narrator: Once upon a time, there was a Sultan who had a beautiful daughter. Her name was Perihan and she was so beautiful that birds would start singing when she walked through the gardens. Princes everywhere wanted to marry her. But the Sultan loved his Perihan very much and he could not choose between the princes.

Stage directions	Script	
Suddenly, he raises his index finger as he has an idea.	**Narrator:**	So one day, he thought of a competition.
He smiles and looks at the audience.	**Sultan:**	The Prince who brings me the most wonderful gift will marry my daughter.
The guard brings in three Princes, (suitors), from stage left who stand in a line. The guard gestures to the 1st suitor that he may now present his gift and so he steps forward. He is holding the bird in a cage in his left hand. He has a confident expression on his face, as if he is certain that the Sultan will choose his gift.	**Narrator:**	When they heard about the competition, Princes from all over the world brought the Sultan strange gifts. One brought a bird with golden feathers.
	Suitor 1:	I have brought this bird! It has got golden feathers!
The Sultan, however, does not raise his arm to receive the gift. He just looks at it carefully and gestures to the suitor to go away.	**Sultan:**	**Hmm. That's very nice, but my gardens are full of beautiful birds that can sing, too. I don't need this golden one.**
The suitor looks very sad and walks back into the line. The guard gestures to the 2nd suitor and he approaches the Sultan carrying a large basket full of colourful eggs with a hen on top. He picks up an egg from the basket and shows it to the Sultan and the audience.	**Narrator:**	The prince left the palace, sadly, carrying the golden bird. Another brought a hen that could lay colourful eggs.
	Suitor 2:	**I have brought this hen! It can lay colourful eggs!**
But the Sultan only laughs and waves him away. The man picks up his gifts and walks back into line, his head lowered.	**Sultan:**	What use do I have for colourful eggs? If I want blue eggs or red eggs, I can just paint them!
The 3rd suitor is carrying a dark blue velvet cushion with a huge diamond star on it. He bows to the Sultan and holds up the diamond. The Sultan gives a big sigh and walks to a treasure chest, stage right, gesturing for the suitor to follow him.	**Narrator:**	Another brought a diamond in the shape of a star and as big as a coconut.
	Suitor 3:	**I have brought this diamond in the shape of a star!**

The Sultan opens the chest and shows the suitor a large pile of treasure.

Narrator: The Sultan took the Prince to a big room, opened the door and the Prince saw sparkling diamonds everywhere.

The Sultan looks bored. The suitor stares at the treasure, his eyes and mouth wide open. The third suitor goes back into the line of suitors.
The guard gestures to the suitors that they must leave. They walk off sadly, heads bowed. The Sultan sits on his throne again and sighs. The guard bows and walks off. Stage lights go off. Curtains close.

Sultan: As you can see, I have more diamonds and precious jewels than I need.
They are all wonderful gifts. But none of them are special enough to let you marry my daughter.

Narrator: And the princes left, sadly.

***Song* - What Can We Offer the Sultan?**

What can we offer the Sultan?
We brought him the best we could find!
But nothing is better than what he has got
We think he is very unkind!

What can we offer the Sultan?
I can't believe what I heard!
He's not impressed with the golden feathers
of my beautiful golden bird!

What can we offer the Sultan?
A magical hen is just great!
If you want red, green or blue eggs,
you've got them right there on your plate!

What can we offer the Sultan,
when diamonds are not good enough?
He's got more than a jewellery shop
and lots of other stuff!

Scene 2

Curtains open. Stage lights go on. The scene shows an open air market. There are three stalls with a merchant behind each one. The three Princes enter stage left. They are each carrying money pouches with gold coins.

The 1st Prince goes to the stall selling mirrors, stage right. The merchant produces a mirror from under the stall.

The Prince smiles and gives him a handful of coins. Then he turns to the audience, proudly showing the magic mirror.

The 2nd Prince goes to the stall selling carpets. The merchant shows him a carpet and gestures with his arm the idea of something taking off and flying in the sky.

The Prince smiles and gives the pouch to the merchant.

He proudly shows his carpet to the audience.

Narrator: In another faraway land, there lived three brothers who were Princes. They, too, heard of Princess Perihan's beauty and they all wanted to marry her. Each of them had five thousand pieces of gold to buy a gift for the Sultan. So they went to a market full of strange things to find gifts.
The first Prince bought a magic mirror. In it you could see what was happening anywhere in the world!

1st Prince: What is so special about this mirror?

Merchant 1: This is a magic mirror! When you look into it, you can see what is happening anywhere in the world!

1st Prince: This is the most wonderful gift of all. Surely the Sultan will let **me** marry his daughter!

Narrator: The second Prince bought a magic carpet. When you sat on it, you could fly anywhere in the world!

2nd Prince: What is so special about this carpet?

Merchant 2: This is a magic carpet! When you sit on it, you can fly anywhere in the world!

2nd Prince: This is a fantastic gift! I will be the one to marry the Princess!

The 3rd Prince notices the lemon stall and walks over to it.

Narrator: In the market, the third Prince, the youngest of all, saw a merchant whom he had never seen before.

The lemon merchant does not look the same as the previous merchants - he is dressed as a beggar. The 3rd Prince picks up a lemon and looks at it carefully.

Merchant 3: Lemons! Lemons!

Narrator: The third Prince was interested and asked the merchant what was special about his lemons.

The 3rd Prince rubs his chin to show that he is thinking hard about whether or not to buy the lemon.

3rd Prince: What is so special about these lemons?

Merchant 3: These are magic lemons. The juice from them will cure any illness!

He steps away from the merchant, stage left, thinking.

Narrator: The merchant told the Prince each lemon cost five thousand pieces of gold. The Prince thought for a long time.

Then he shrugs his shoulders, goes back to the merchant and gives him his money pouch and takes one lemon.
He goes back to his brothers who are still standing with the carpet and the mirror, centre stage.

3rd Prince: Maybe this gift will be the one the Sultan likes.

Narrator: And he paid five thousand pieces of gold for one small lemon!

***Song* - The Best Gift For Love**

With a magic mirror,
you can see your true love's face,
even if they're far away
in another place.

The magic carpet takes you
to your true love's heart –
in just a minute you are there,
no matter how far apart.

A magic lemon cures you
and makes all sick things well.
Which of these gifts is the best,
I wonder? Can you tell?

Drama Activities

1 First-time listening and reading

Aims: To familiarise Ss with the story they are going to perform.

Preparation: Read the story and decide at which points it would be suitable to stop and ask Ss to speculate on the story.

Materials: The audio cassette or CD and the Pupil's book.

Description:

1. Introduce the story to the Ss by showing them the Pupil's Book cover and front page. Point to the characters and ask for Ss' speculations on both story and characters.
2. Play the recording while Ss follow in their books. When you reach the first stopping point, ask Ss to close their books and tell you what they think is going to happen next. Accept all answers and then continue.
3. After listening to the development of the story, stop again and ask Ss which of their suggestions were correct. Then play the story until the next stopping point. Repeat until the story is complete.

2 Listen for the cue

Aims: To help Ss learn their lines and identify when to say them.

Preparation: Cut out the script pages in the Pupil's Books.

Materials: The scripts from the Pupil's Book.

Description:

1. Point out that knowing when to speak is important in a play and that in order to do that, they should identify the lines of the characters who speak before them (i.e. the cues).
2. Allocate the roles and ask Ss to underline their lines in one colour and circle the lines before them. Ss who are not willing to act can work as prompters.
3. Ask Ss to read out the play. Prompters can help out those who confuse their lines.
4. You can repeat the reading, focusing on intonation, pronunciation, clarity etc.

3 Mirrors

Aims: To encourage Ss' observation and concentration abilities.

Preparation: None.

Materials: None.

Description:

1 Ask Ss to sit or stand in pairs facing each other. Explain that one of them, S A, has to act as if he/she is looking in a mirror, and the other, S B, has to 'mirror' their exact movements.

2 Ss start practising in pairs. After a few minutes, ask Ss to change roles and S B takes over the lead while S A 'mirrors' the movements. Point out that concentration is important and monitor the class, watching each pair.

3 This activity can be turned into a game, where the best pair wins, by eliminating pairs if they do not mirror the exact movements of their partners.

4 Sound effects

Aims: To help Ss to use their voices to the full range and to help avoid embarrassment when using their voices beyond the normal range.

Preparation: Decide on a story which may have a lot of sound effects such as a walk in the park, a visit to the zoo etc.

Materials: None.

Description:

1 Ask the Ss to make the loudest/quietest/highest/lowest/shortest/longest noises they can with their voices in a group.

2 Ask the Ss to make repeated sounds using their tonges and lips (a) with voice ie. b-b-b, m-m-m, d-d-d, g-g-g, j-j-j, l-l-l, n-n-n, w-w-w, v-v-v, y-y-y, z-z-z, a-a-a, e-e-e, i-i-i, o-o-o, u-u-u and (b) without voice ie. k-k-k, f-f-f, h-h-h, p-p-p, s-s-s, t-t-t, (Some letters of the alphabet have been omitted because they are compound sounds or have different sounds in different words).

3 The teacher describes the walk/visit etc and stops at appropriate times to wait for the sound effect.

4 Record some of the sessions for future reference.

5 You are walking through...

Aims:

1 To encourage Ss to exaggerate action for the benefit of an audience.

2 To help Ss associate action with the words being spoken.

3 To encourage Ss to use their bodies to enchance the action and to lose inhibition when performing.

Preparation: None

Materials: None

Description:

1 Ask Ss to form a large circle. Join in to help them to picture the scene they are to mime.

2 Ask everyone to walk in the same direction around the available space at a normal pace.

3 Change the scene by saying "*You are walking through thick, sticky mud.*" Immediately the Ss' movements should change to fit the new scene. They should change the way they move their feet and their facial expressions, pretending to be struggling and to be uncertain of where they are putting their feet.

4 After a lap of the circle, change the scene again. Some examples include:
You are walking on the moon.
You are walking through thick grass.
You are walking on hot coals.
You are walking on quicksand.
You are walking on clouds.
You are walking on sticky bubble gum.

6 Obvious observing

Aims: To encourage Ss to concentrate on what is happening on stage and pick up action cues.

Preparation: None.

Materials: None.

Description:

1 Split the class into pairs. Have them stand facing each other and observe each other closely.

2 After a short time, have the partners turn their backs on each other and make changes to their personal appearance (change hair, move a ring to a different finger, unbutton a sleeve etc).

3 Let them observe each other again and try to identify the changes.

4 Repeat the process with different numbers of changes and/or longer or shorter observation time.

7 Name the props

Aims: To help Ss identify the props they will be using and become aware of their uses and qualities.

Preparation: The props used in the play set out at the front of the classroom.

Materials: The props from the play.

Description:

1 Name all the props, one by one and ask Ss to repeat after you.

2 Tell Ss that you are thinking about one of the props and they must guess which one.

3 Ss should not call out the names of the props, but should ask questions about its colour, use, shape etc.

4 The S who guesses correctly comes to the front and takes over from the teacher.

8 Changing channels

Aims:

1 To encourage Ss to use body language and facial expressions when acting.

2 To encourage Ss to work together when on stage.

Preparation: Make a list of different types of TV programmes your Ss might watch on TV, e.g. *a comedy, a very sad story, the news, a detective story, a soap opera, a children's programme, a music programme, a western, a documentary* etc.

Materials: A large empty cardboard box to use as a TV set and any kind of remote control.

Description:

1 Ask Ss what types of TV programmes they normally watch on TV. Write them on a list on the board and add any more from your own list.

2 Put the 'TV set' on your desk and ask Ss to move their chairs in front of it, and sit around it as if they are watching.

3 'Turn on' the TV and choose one of the programmes on your list. Say *"You are watching a comedy"*. Ss need to act accordingly, laughing, moving about in their chairs etc. After a while, 'change the channel' saying *"You are watching a very sad story"*. Ss should change their expression and posture.

4 Continue 'changing channels' until Ss have practised all programme types on your list or until they are relaxed and ready to start rehearsing the play you are about to stage.

Word List

The words in colour are presented in the picture dictionary of the main story.

about
after
again
all over
another
anything
anywhere
arms
ask
be (was/were)
beautiful
beauty
bed
bedside
before
begin (began)
believe
between
big
birds
blue
both
bring (brought)
brothers
buy (bought)
call
can (could)
carpet
carry
cheeks
choose (chose)
coconut
colourful
come (came)
competition
cost (cost)
cry (cried)
cup
cure
day
daughter
diamond
die
doctor
door
each

eggs
enough
ever after
everywhere
eyes
fail
fantastic
faraway
feathers
find (found)
first
five thousand
fly (flew)
flying
follow
full
gardens
get (got)
get up (got up)
gift
give (gave)
go (went)
gold
golden
good (better - best)
hall

happen
happily
hear (heard)
help
hen
here
hug
just
ill
illness
interested
interesting
jewels
journey
juice
jump onto
know (knew)
land
laugh
leave (left)
lemon
let (let)
lie (lay)
life
like
live

long
look into
look like
love
magic
majesty
market
marry (married)
maybe
merchant
minute
mirror
much
name
need
never
next day
nice
none
now
once upon a time
one day
open
paint
palace
palace doors
pay (paid)
pieces of gold
pink
poor
precious
prince
princess
quick
red
right
room
royal
run - ran
sadly
same
save
say (said)
second
see (saw)
shape
should
shout
simple
sing (sang)
sit (sat)
small

sofa
sparkling
special
squeeze
star
start
step forward
strange
strange things
Sultan
surely
take (took)
talk
tell (told)
thank you
think (thought)
third
through
time
try (tried)
turn to
unroll
use
very
walk
want
well
win (won)
wonderful
world
young